S0-BTR-730

Hotchkiss Public Library
WITHDRAWN
PO Box 540   NOV 07
Hotchkiss, CO 81419

21st
Century
Skills Library

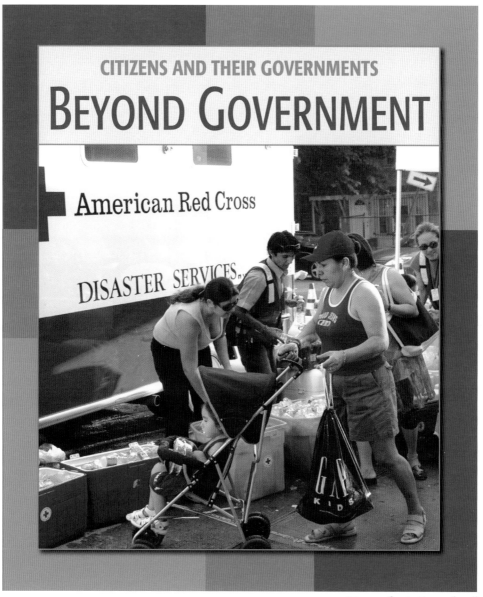

CITIZENS AND THEIR GOVERNMENTS

BEYOND GOVERNMENT

American Red Cross

DISASTER SERVICES

Frank Muschal

Cherry Lake Publishing
Ann Arbor, Michigan

CHERRY LAKE
Publishing

Published in the United States of America by Cherry Lake Publishing
Ann Arbor, MI
www.cherrylakepublishing.com

Photo Credits: Cover, © Zhao Peng/Xinhua Press/CORBIS; Page 12, © Mika/zefa/CORBIS;
Page 15, © John Norris/Corbis; Page 16, Vic Yepello/Star Ledger/CORBIS; Page 18, ©
Chris Faytok/Star Ledger/CORBIS; Page 26, ©Gunter Marx Photography/CORBIS

Copyright ©2008 by Cherry Lake Publishing
All rights reserved. No part of this book may be reproduced or utilized in any
form or by any means without written permission from the publisher.

Library of Congress Cataloging-in-Publication Data
Muschal, Frank.
  Beyond government/by Frank Muschal.
    p. cm.—(Citizens and their governments)
  ISBN-13: 978-1-60279-060-5
  ISBN-10: 1-60279-060-4
  1. Child volunteers—United States—Juvenile literature. 2.
Voluntarism—United States—Juvenile literature. I. Title. II. Series.
  HQ784.V64M87 2008
  361.7'20830973—dc22   2007006337

*Cherry Lake Publishing would like to acknowledge the work of
The Partnership for 21st Century Skills.
Please visit www.21stcenturyskills.org for more information.*

TABLE OF CONTENTS

CHAPTER ONE

Do You Want To Be a Hero?

The fire department is a key service of local governments across the nation.

Our government does many things for us. Local government provides

police and fire protection. The national government prints our money,

runs the national parks, and controls the military. All together, the various

levels of government do much to make our lives safer and better. However,

there are many things that just make our lives *nicer* that government can't or doesn't do. The government doesn't deliver meals to old folks who can't get out. The government doesn't pick up trash along many country roads. The government doesn't take the blind lady grocery shopping. But you could. Doing any one of these would make you a hero.

Perhaps you dream about saving a drowning child or leading a family out of a blazing building. These types of situations don't occur often. That's why we read about them in newspapers. There are other types of heroes, though. You pass them on the street every day without even realizing it.

Young people can be heroes by cleaning up neighborhoods, parks, and playgrounds.

Life & Career Skills

One big problem for all volunteer organizations is people who quit after only a few weeks. Don't become one of these short-timers! Ask if you can observe several meetings or take on a task that is of a short duration. Decide if you can give the time that is needed and be a loyal volunteer.

Heroes don't have to risk their lives to rescue others. They just need to give something of themselves to make other people's lives better. In 2006, more than 65 million **volunteers** in the United States donated their time to their communities. Most, but not nearly all, were adults. For example, some 15.5 million young people in 2004 gave more than a *billion* hours of service to others.

So many good projects need volunteers that you should have no trouble finding one that fits your interests, talents, and schedule. You might start by talking to someone at your church, mosque, or synagogue. Ask specifically for suggestions of programs that need help. If any of the programs interest you, attend several of them as an observer to be sure that you would like help out.

If your church doesn't have any programs that interest you, look around your community. Contact the Salvation Army or the Red Cross in your area. For example, the Red Cross helps people when disaster, such as fire or flood, strikes. The Red Cross collects most of the blood that is used for transfusions in America, too. The Red Cross also runs a variety of classes for young people. These include swimming, babysitting, and first aid. All Red Cross projects use volunteers.

21st Century Content

Because the need for volunteers and help is so great, there are now groups that train people to start their own nonprofit organizations. Most of these are funded by government or charitable grants, so training is free.

CHAPTER TWO

HELP SENIOR CITIZENS

*Meals on Wheels and similar agencies make sure
elderly residents have the meals they need.*

Senior citizens often have many interesting stories to tell, but few people

to listen. Some seniors are no longer fit and their grownup children have

moved away. They live alone and have difficulty doing chores around their homes. One organization that helps them is called

Meals on Wheels. It provides hot meals several days a

week and a friendly ear to listen for a few minutes.

Other seniors have chosen to live in retirement

homes. One of these is the Bethesda Home and

Retirement Center in Chicago. Residents like to talk

with each other, but they rarely have younger people

to talk with. So Bethesda invites "grandchildren" to

adopt "grandparents." The time **commitment** is just

one hour a week. Volunteer "grandchildren" learn a

lot from their adopted grandparents, and they meet

other volunteers, too.

Learning & Innovation Skills

Talking to seniors is an opportunity to learn about life in the past. Ask older adults about their childhoods. What toys were popular? What did they do for fun? Where did their families go on vacation?

Volunteer groups have found that animals help lift the spirits of most people—including older folks.

One thing many senior citizens miss is animal companionship. Many had cats or dogs for most of their lives but are no longer able to care for a pet. The act of simply petting an animal gives anyone—older people included—the opportunity to give affection to another living creature.

Being around pets can also have a good effect on health! Studies have shown that people who own pets often benefit from lower blood pressure.

The Guild Home for the Aged Blind in Yonkers, New York, is a home for people who are without sight as well as being elderly. The Guild Home invites people with gentle pets to bring in their animals for residents to love. The feeling of a wet tongue, a wagging tail, or a gentle purr is all the more delightful to people who have lost their vision.

Like almost all people, older folks enjoy spending some time with pets, too.

CHAPTER THREE

HELP THE DISABLED AND LESS FORTUNATE

*Some programs help disabled participants ride,
care for, and bond with horses.*

Disabled people often have limited opportunities, so a program called

Extraordinary People in Powder Springs, Georgia, tries to improve the

situation. It gives disabled people the chance to ride horses. The program uses volunteers to lead the horses and to stay beside

them and make sure the rider remains centered in the

saddle. Volunteers also care for the horses as well as

help keep the barn, stalls, and aisles clean.

In Shoreline, Washington, a program called

Stepping Out for Fun pairs volunteers aged 14 to

65 with people who suffer from Down syndrome,

autism, and similar problems. Once a month, the

two new friends go out for fun activities. Stepping

Out for Fun often hosts some of the activities

for little or no money. More importantly, both

participants enjoy themselves.

Down syndrome is a genetic disorder that occurs in about 1 out of every 1,000 births. Autism is becoming much more common and may occur as often as in 1 out of every 150 births.

Learning & Innovation Skills

Bingo cards can be printed in Braille, a system of raised dots on paper that can be "read" by touching them. What other games do you think could be adapted for visually impaired people? What changes would need to be made?

In San Jose, California, the Santa Clara Valley Blind Center offers various activities to its vision-impaired members. One of these is a weekly bingo tournament. Volunteers call out the numbers and help members fill up their bingo cards. The center also offers crafts classes, socials, exercise groups, and outdoor activities, all of which use volunteers.

Sometimes, people with impaired vision need help with everyday living such as grocery shopping. Many organizations provide volunteers to help them do these tasks. In Wisconsin, volunteers with the Badger Association of the Blind and Visually Impaired accompany people who have trouble seeing

In addition to helping with basic needs, volunteers help visually impaired people with recreational activities and other ways to improve their quality of life.

as they run their errands. Sometimes the volunteer must be able to drive,

but often walking is all that is necessary.

These youngsters help deliver food to a needy family.

Many organizations in America provide food to people who need it.

One of them is called Second Harvest. It collects food from food drives

and donations. Volunteers sort the food and pack it into boxes so that each

box contains enough to feed a senior citizen or a mother and child for a month. Older volunteers are needed to deliver the food, but Second Harvest accepts volunteers as young as 14 if they are accompanied by an adult.

Heifer International provides **livestock, poultry,** and training to needy families around the world. The animals are raised for the offspring and the food they provide, such as milk and eggs. With this beginning, the family can become **self-reliant** instead of depending on others for food. Families that receive the animals agree to share any offspring with other needy families. This way, even more people can prosper.

21st Century Content

In 2006, students at Charles Armstrong Middle School in Belmont, California, raised cash by doing odd jobs in their community. They used the money to purchase 2 water buffalo, 2 pigs, and 13 flocks of baby chickens for the Heifer Project. The project is an international effort to feed the hungry through sustainable resources. There are programs in Africa, Asia, the South Pacific, Eastern Europe, and many more places.

Many high schools now include a community service requirement.
This student is a member of a club that worked with Habitat
for Humanity to build this house in New Jersey.

Some people need homes as well as food, and a program called Habitat for Humanity helps with that. Since its founding in 1976, the program has built more than 200,000 homes around the world, including in all 50 states of the United States as well as more than 90 other nations. The program uses volunteers to help raise money for projects as well as build the homes. The families that get the finished homes, including the kids, work on the construction, too.

Learning & Innovation Skills

There are hundreds of homeless shelters in America, in virtually every state and big city, and these provide emergency homes for growing numbers of families. What could you do to help the homeless in your community?

CHAPTER FOUR

HELP ANIMALS AND THE ENVIRONMENT

There are many volunteer opportunities for young people at local animal shelters such as this one.

Many volunteers are needed to work with animals. The North Shore Animal League America in Port Washington, New York is one such place. They have volunteer opportunities for everyone from teenagers to senior citizens. Newborn kittens and puppies need to be fed. Cages need to be cleaned. Dogs need to be walked. After Hurricanes

Katrina and Rita, the League rescued more than

1,400 pets that needed attention and helped in

reuniting with their owners.

Pets are not the only kinds of animals that

sometimes need help from humans. Birds of prey,

such as hawks or falcons, may be found wounded.

A baby owl may be orphaned or abandoned by its

parents. Sometimes, birds just get too old to hunt

for themselves. There are nature centers that care for

these animals. There are also huge volunteer needs

when there is an oil spill. Birds can't fly with the

sticky, heavy oil on their bodies.

After a tremendous oil spill off the coast of France in January of 2000, volunteers tried to rescue more than 60,000 birds that had been coated with oil. Hard work rescued many of the affected birds.

Caring for injured hawks, raptors, eagles, and falcons can be rewarding to both the bird and the people who aid it.

In North Carolina, the Carolina Raptor Center cares for birds of prey.

It houses birds that have been injured too badly to be released back into

the wild. Besides caring for the birds, the center educates the public about

the role of raptors in nature. Volunteers help maintain the grounds, greet

visitors, answer questions, and do general office work.

Volunteering to Help the Environment

Sometimes wild animals can be helped by helping to preserve their habitats. In earlier days, people often tried to change natural habitats into something they thought would be more pleasing or useful. Now we are beginning to understand the negative impact that all that change has had on our modern environment. Efforts across the country are underway to restore many habitats to their natural state.

Kudzu is a Japanese vine that was first brought to the U.S. in 1876 and grows well in the American Southeast. It has overwhelmed some habitats there.

21st Century Content

Everglades National Park is one of the United States' unique national sites. Some 27 kinds of snakes and more than 50 types of butterflies live there—along with manatees, panthers, vultures, alligators, and billions and billions of mosquitoes. Similar unique parks exist around the world, such as Namibia's Etosha National Park, the Fundacíon Jocotoco Reserves of Ecuador, and others on every continent. Volunteers in all countries are helping to preserve nature.

In Florida, volunteers with the Everglades **Restoration** Movement are helping to preserve and restore this unique national park. Volunteers work to eradicate non-native trees that are destroying native species that animals use for food and shelter. The main culprit is a tree called the melaleuca, which has no natural enemies in Florida. Volunteers work with government groups to saw down and remove the melaleucas.

America's heartland was once covered with vast prairies. Native grasses provided food and shelter for the countless animals. In the 1800s, pioneers plowed up the native grasses and planted other crops. Now,

Volunteers are working to restore prairie habitats in Illinois,
Wisconsin, Minnesota, and elsewhere.

large areas are being turned back into prairies. For example, volunteers

with the Johnson County Conservation Board in southeastern Iowa cut

brush, collect seeds, and replant native vegetation every year.

CHAPTER FIVE

HELP THE COMMUNITY

*Volunteers can help at many community events, such as
handing out water at running events and triathlons.*

Some of the most fun volunteer activities may be ones in your community. For example, it takes many volunteers to put on a successful marathon. Volunteers have to register the runners, set up the road barriers, put up neighborhood signs about the event, hand out water during the race, and maybe even clean up afterward. Volunteers also have to determine the winners and hand out the awards. Now that's fun!

Volunteers also help with local band concerts, plays, and talent shows. They put up advertising posters, sell tickets, set out chairs, make costumes, and show audience members to their seats.

Life & Career Skills

There are thousands of museums in the United States, and almost all of them need volunteers. The museums cover everything from art and musical instruments to wine, railroads, surfing, airplanes, history, wildlife, TVs, and just about anything you can think of. Why do people enjoy volunteering at museums?

Many museums use volunteers to conduct tours for visitors. Often these volunteers must agree to spend several hours learning about the museum and practicing their talks. Other museum volunteers may staff the gift shop and front desk. They may even make the displays of fresh flowers that are sitting around.

In many communities, groups have joined the "Adopt-A-Road" program. Group members are responsible for keeping a specific section of a roadway free of litter.

There are many ways to be a hero even if you don't get a medal. The activities and the organizations mentioned in this book are just a tiny sampling of the many, many opportunities. However, you must decide what you want to volunteer for. What talents do you have? What are your interests? Whom do you want to help? Be someone's hero. You can make a difference, now and throughout your life.

It can be easy to find a volunteer opportunity that fits you. First, you need to be sure you have the time and commitment. Then you can search online—or in the telephone book—for agencies that match volunteers with the organizations that need their help.

GLOSSARY

commitment (kuh-MIT-muhnt) obligation or pledge to do something

habitats (HAB-i-tats) areas or environments where an animal normally lives

livestock (LAHYV-stok) animals such as cattle or horses raised for profit, often on a farm

poultry (POHL-tree) birds such as chickens and turkeys raised for meat or eggs

self-reliant (self ri-LAHY-uhnt) trusting one's own powers or judgment

restoration (res-tuh-REY-shuhn) process of returning to original condition

volunteers (vol-uhn-TEERZ) people who do something of their own free will and without payment

For More Information

Books

Ditchfield, Christin. *Serving Your Community*.
New York: Scholastic, 2004.

Francis, Dorothy. *Clara Barton*. Brookfield, CT: Millbrook Press, 2002.

Isler, Claudia. *Volunteering to Help With Animals*.
New York: Rosen Book Works, 2000.

Lewis, Barbara A. *The Kid's Guide to Service Projects*.
Minneapolis, MN: Free Spirit Publishing, 1995.

Lewis, Barbara A. *The Kid's Guide to Social Action*.
Minneapolis, MN: Free Spirit Publishing, 1998.

Newell, Patrick. *Volunteering to Help Seniors*.
New York: Rosen Book Works, 2000.

Perry, Susan K. *Catch the Spirit: Teen Volunteers Tell How They Made a Difference*. New York: Franklin Watts, 2000.

Other Media

To find out more about the American Red Cross and its
volunteer opportunities, go to *http://www.redcross.org/*

To learn more about Habitat for Humanity,
go to *http://www.habitat.org/*

INDEX

ABOUT THE AUTHOR

Frank Muschal lives in Chicago with his elderly cat, Agatha. ("She's older than laptops and cell phones, but I'm older than TV.") He's been writing and editing for textbook publishers for thirty years and has no guilt feelings about tormenting students all that time. Besides writing, Frank keeps busy playing tennis, riding horses, and fumbling around on his guitar. "I'm no rock star," he says. "I just want to make me more interesting to myself."